90 DAY BIBLE

New Testament
Reading Plan

———

Mike Baker

Jim
Thank you for your friendship
& encouragement
Never fear!
Psalm 27:1

Mike Baker

To my wonderful wife, Carla.

All Scripture is given my inspiration of God, and is profitable for doctrine, for reproof, for correction, for instruction in righteousness, that the man of God may be complete, thoroughly equipped for every good work.

2 Timothy 3:16-17

Table of Contents

Introduction

Thank you for your interest in reading the Bible! This reading plan covers the entire New Testament in 90 days. Each day will cover 2 or 3 chapters which will only take 10-15 minutes to read.

You may use choose any version of the Bible to use with this plan. All terms and Scriptures used here are from the New King James Version. Reading can be done online, from a printed Bible, tablet or phone. Find what works best for you.

Before jumping in to read the assigned chapters, take a minute to read through the entire page. First, you will find a list of two or three defined terms, one for each chapter that day. These definitions are of the Greek words in the text, so they may differ slightly from a simple English definition. A list of all words with Strong's numbers are available in the back if you want to research them on your own.

Next, one question per chapter is provided. By reviewing the questions in advance, you will be able to read for specific content. Be sure to write in your answers.

Finally, a daily memory verse is provided. Meditate on this verse and commit it to memory. Some may find it helpful to keep a journal and write down the memory verse each day.

Invite others to join you in this reading plan. Discuss your reading with family, friends or a class.

Additional recourses are available at 90DayBiblePlan.com. These include suggested topics and resources for classes or sermons based on the weekly reading as well as other helpful information. Other books are scheduled in this series which will cover the Old Testament.

When completed with this book, you will have read 260 chapters, learned 260 words, answered 260 questions and established a good habit for regular Bible reading. That's quite an accomplishment.

Good job! Now, let's get to work on day 1.

Date started reading: _____

Day 1
Matthew 1-3

Terms to know
Genealogy: Genesis, lineage, generations of ancestors.

Magi: Name for priests and wise men among the Medes, Persians and Babylonians. Specialized in the study of astrology and enchantment.

Baptize: To dip, immerse, submerge for a religious purpose.

Questions
1. List the 5 women in Matthew's genealogy of Jesus.

2. Who warned Joseph to flee to Egypt?

3. Why was Jesus baptized?

Memory verse: Matthew 1:21
And she will bring forth a Son, and you shall call His name Jesus, for He will save His people from their sins.

Day 2
Matthew 4-6

Terms to know
Tempt: Try, prove, put to the test.

Blessed: Fortunate one, happy, possessing the favor of God.

Alms: Charity, money given to the poor.

Questions
1. What were the three temptations of Jesus?

2. What two purposes are gained by letting our light shine?

3. Where will your heart be?

Memory verse: Matthew 6:24
No one can serve two masters; for either he will hate the one and love the other, or else he will be loyal to the one and despise the other. You cannot serve God and mammon.

Day 3
Matthew 7-9

Terms to know
Scribe: A writer, often well-versed in the Law of Moses, able to expound on the Law.

Leper: A scale, leprous, one who has the disease of leprosy.

Fast: To abstain from eating.

Questions
1. How will you know false prophets?

2. Why was the centurion's faith so great?

3. List the different maladies Jesus healed.

Memory verse: Matthew 7:12
Therefore, whatever you want men to do to you, do also to them, for this is the Law and the Prophets.

Day 4
Matthew 10-12

Terms to know

Apostle: One sent, ambassador. In the New Testament generally in reference to the twelve.

Yoke: Serving to couple two things together, e.g., cattle. Metaphorically, any bondage or burden of laws as used in Matt. 11.

Sabbath: Rest, a cessation from labor. Jewish Sabbath, seventh day of the week.

Questions

1. What are the names of the 12 apostles?

2. Why did Jesus rebuke Chorazin, Bethsaida and Capernaum?

3. Who are Jesus' mother and brothers?

Memory verse: Matthew 10:32
Therefore, whoever confesses Me before men, him I will also confess before My Father who is in heaven.

Day 5
Matthew 13-15

Terms to know

Parable: A placing side by side, a comparison, similitude. A story cast alongside to demonstrate a point.

Tetrarch: A ruler of a fourth part of a district or province.

Transgress: Beyond or contrary to, to violate. In the New Testament it always has a moral sense.

Questions

1. What are the names of the brothers of Jesus?

2. Why was John the Baptist in prison?

3. How much food was taken up after feeding the four thousand?

Memory verse: Matthew 15:4
Let them alone. They are blind leaders of the blind. And if the blind leads the blind, both will fall into a ditch.

Day 6
Matthew 16-18

Terms to know
Pharisee: A sect of the Jews that considered themselves better than others and who were very zealous for the traditions of their elders.

Transfigured: To transform, change one's form.

Forgive: To let go from one's power, possession, to let go free, escape.

Questions
1. Who are the ones Jesus said would cause Him to suffer and be killed?

2. Why could the disciples not cast out the demon from a boy?

3. What are the three steps to take concerning a brother who sins against you?

Memory verse: Matthew 16:26
For what profit is it to a man if he gains the whole world and loses his own soul? Or what will a man give in exchange for his soul?

Day 7
Matthew 19-21

Terms to know

Sexual immorality: To commit fornication, or any sexual sin; fornication, lewdness.

Denarius: A Roman penny equivalent in value to the Greek Drachma. Widely circulated in the Roman empire. About a day's wage.

Hosanna: Save now, help now, or save we pray thee. Later a form of wishing safety and prosperity.

Questions

1. What did the rich young ruler value above following Jesus?

2. What did Jesus predict that the Gentiles would do to Him prior to His resurrection??

3. Why did Jesus drive out people from the temple?

Memory verse: Matthew 19:24
And again I say to you, it is easier for a camel to go through the eye of a needle than for a rich man to enter the kingdom of God.

End of Week 1

Congratulations on finishing the first week of reading. Please use this page to write down people, events or teaching from the reading that you would like to learn more about. Share these with your family, small group, teacher or preacher and learn about them together. Some examples are below for this first week.

For further study

- What can we learn from the temptation of Jesus?
- How can we learn to pray for our enemies?

Day 8
Matthew 22-24

Terms to know
Sadducee: A sect of the Jews in opposition to the Pharisees and Essenes. A smaller party that only accepted the teachings of Moses, denied the resurrection of man.

Phylacteries: Pouches or boxes containing scrolls or parchments on which the Jews wrote certain portions of the law and bound them to their foreheads and wrists.

Christ: Messiah, anointed one.

Questions
1. Why were the Sadducees asking Jesus questions about resurrections?

2. Why did the scribes and Pharisees do their works?

3. What will false Christs use to deceive others?

Memory verse: Matthew 24:35
Heaven and earth will pass away, but My words will by no means pass away.

17

Day 9
Matthew 25-27

Terms to know

Talent: Used as a commercial weight, equaled sixty minas or 6,000 drachmae. The Jewish talent contained 3,000 shekels or 113 pounds.

Remission: To release one's sins from the sinner, forgiveness, to remit.

Crucified: To impale on a cross, punishment by crucifixion, affix or nail to a cross. Romans used this method of punishment extensively.

Questions

1. Why did the one talent servant hide the money?

2. How much did Judas receive for betraying Jesus?

3. Why did Pilate set a guard at the tomb of Jesus?

Memory verse: Matthew 27:37
And they put up over His head the accusation written against Him: THIS IS JESUS THE KING OF THE JEWS.

Day 10
Matthew 28 – Mark 2

Terms to know
Disciple: To learn, to understand a pupil, generally followers of Jesus, also spoken of as the 12 apostles.

Synagogue: A Jewish place of assembly, worship.

Paralytic: Palsied, nervous affliction denoting loss of motor power in the muscles.

Questions
1. What were the guards paid to say about the empty tomb?

2. What was the consequence of the healed leper telling others what Jesus did?

3. What extra effort did the four friends of the paralytic man perform?

Memory verse: Matthew 28:19-20
Go therefore and make disciples of all the nations, baptizing them in the name of the Father and of the Son and of the Holy Spirit, teaching them to observe all that I have commanded you; and lo, I am with you always even to the end of the age. Amen.

Day 11
Mark 3-5

Terms to know

Beelzebub: Lord of flies or fly-god. Used in the day of Jesus as a title of Satan as the prince of demons.

Wayside: A place, way street. Hardened pathway.

Demon: Unclean, wicked or evil spirit.

Questions

1. What is the unpardonable sin?

2. What causes a thorny ground hearer to not be faithful?

3. Who was allowed to be with Jesus when He raised Jairus' daughter from the dead?

Memory verse: Mark 4:34
But without a parable He did not speak to them. And when they were alone, He explained all things to His disciples.

Day 12
Mark 6-8

Terms to know
Work: A worthy deed, sign or miracle.

Corban: A gift or an offering dedicated to God. This gift was used to excuse a person from their duty toward their own parents by committing a future gift to the temple.

Sign: Mark, token, miracle with a spiritual end and purpose.

Questions
1. Why had the disciples not understood about the loaves in the feeding of the 5,000?

2. By holding to the traditions of men what had the people done to God's commandments?

3. How long had the people been with Jesus without eating?

Memory verse: Mark 8:34
Whoever desires to come after Me, let him deny himself, and take up his cross, and follow Me.

Day 13
Mark 9-11

Terms to know

Millstone: A grinding stone, stone from a mill.

Adultery: Fornication involving a married partner with someone outside of the marriage.

Rabbi: A doctor, teacher, mentor, a title of honor in the Jewish schools.

Questions

1. What will happen to the one who desires to be the greatest?

2. What did Peter leave in order to follow Jesus?

3. What did the people spread on the road ahead of Jesus?

Memory verse: Mark 10:45
For even the Son of Man did not come to be served, but to serve, and to give His life a ransom for many.

Day 14
Mark 12-14

Terms to know

Mite: A small coin, the smallest coin in use among the Jews. Equal to half a farthing.

Deceive: To cause to wander, lead astray, to cause to err.

Blasphemy: Verbal abuse against someone, spiritually against or toward God.

Questions

1. Why had the widow given more than the rich givers?

2. Why did Jesus tell the apostles not to worry about what to say when arrested?

3. What happened to the apostles when Jesus was arrested?

Memory verse: Mark 14:38
Watch and pray, lest you enter into temptation. The spirit indeed is willing, but the flesh is weak.

23

End of Week 2

Congratulations on finishing another week of reading. Please use this page to write down people, events or teaching from the reading that you would like to learn more about. Share these with your family, small group, teacher or preacher and learn about them together.

For further study

Day 15
Mark 15 – Luke 1

Terms to know
Praetorium: A house or palace of a governor of a province. The court or part of the palace where the procurator's guards were stationed.

Rebuked: To reproach someone for something, to upbraid, chide.

Prophesied: To foretell things to come.

Questions
1. What crime did Barabbas commit?

2. How did the apostles confirm the word they preached?

3. What happened to Zacharias since he did not believe the words of Gabriel?

Memory verse: Luke 1:37
For with God nothing will be impossible.

Day 16
Luke 2-4

Terms to know
Betrothed: To ask in marriage, to be engaged. Before an actual marriage, a groom would enter into an agreement with the bride's family with an irrevocable contract and payment of a mohar. From that point until a future marriage ceremony, the bride was betrothed and could not be given to another without receiving a certificate of divorce.

Repentance: A change of mind from evil to good.

Anointed: To daub, smear, anoint with oil, chosen, consecrated, set apart for service.

Questions
1. What had to happen before Simeon would die?

2. What was John's response to the tax collectors?

3. In what city did Jesus read from the prophet Isaiah?

Memory verse: Luke 2:49
Why did you seek me? Did you not know that I must be about My Father's business?

Day 17
Luke 5-7

Terms to know
Publican: A reaper of the taxes or customs. Objects of bitter hatred and scorn by the Jews due to their unfair practices.

Merciful: To pity, have compassion upon.

Glutton: an excessive or unrestrained eater.

Questions
1. Why did the scribes and Pharisees object to Jesus eating at Matthew's house?

2. How did the sick people seek to receive the healing power of Jesus?

3. Why did the centurion not want Jesus to come to his house?

Memory verse: Luke 6:36
Therefore be merciful, just as your Father also is merciful.

Day 18
Luke 8-10

Terms to know

Perishing: To destroy fully, or cause to lose or die.

Implore: To make one's need known, to beseech.

Samaritan: Inhabitant of Samaria, settlers in Samaria when the Israelites were in exile. Severe animosity existed between the Jews and Samaritans. To call someone a Samaritan was a term of reproach or contempt.

Questions

1. Where did the demon-possessed man live?

2. What were the disciples to do to a city that would not receive them?

3. What brought joy to the disciples who returned to Jesus?

Memory verse: Luke 9:62
No one, having put his hand to the plow, and looking back, is fit for the kingdom of God.

Day 19
Luke 11-13

Terms to know
Persistence: Impudent, recklessness or disregard of consideration by the one making the request.

Covetousness: Greediness, to wish to have more.

Adversary: To oppose, to set oneself against.

Questions
1.   Why were the people of Nineveh qualified to judge the generation during Jesus' day?

2.   The rich farmer left God out of his life. How many personal pronouns did he use in Luke 12:16-19?

3.   What did Jesus call Herod?

Memory verse: Luke 12:8-9
Also I say to you, whoever confesses Me before men, him the Son of Man also will confess before the angels of God. But he who denies Me before men will be denied before the angels of God.

Day 20
Luke 14-16

Terms to know
Dropsy: Hydropic, dropsical, a condition of excessive accumulation of serious fluids in the body.

Prodigal: Profligately, riotously, dissolutely, wasteful.

Steward: An administrator, a person who manages the domestic affairs of a family, business or minor. A house manager, overseer.

Questions
1. What were the three excuses given for the great supper?

2. What position was the prodigal son willing to take upon his return?

3. Why did the rich man want someone to go to his brothers?

Memory verse: Luke 14:11
For whoever exalts himself will be humbled, and he who humbles himself will be exalted.

Day 21
Luke 17-19

Terms to know
Offend: To cause to stumble and fall, a cause of entrapment.

Justified: Set forth as righteous, to make innocent as a judicial act.

Austere: Honor, meaning earnest and severe.

Questions
1. What two actions are we to do with those who sin against us?

2. What did the judge fear from the widow?

3. Where did the servant hide his one mina?

Memory verse: Luke 17:3
Take heed to yourselves. If your brother sins against you, rebuke him; and if he repents, forgive him.

End of Week 3

Congratulations on finishing another week of reading. Please use this page to write down people, events or teaching from the reading that you would like to learn more about. Share these with your family, small group, teacher or preacher and learn about them together.

For further study

Day 22
Luke 20-22

Terms to know

Cornerstone: Corner of a building, spiritually Christ is the chief cornerstone.

Carousing: The sense of disgust and loathing from an overindulgence of wine.

Passover: An exemption, immunity, a festival of the Jews in commemoration of God's sparing the Jews with the destruction of the firstborn in Egypt. Celebrated the 14th day of Nisan.

Questions

1. Why will the scribes receive greater condemnation?

2. Where did Jesus go at night after teaching in the temple by day?

3. What happened when Peter denied Jesus the third time?

Memory verse: Luke 20:25
Render therefore to Caesar the things that are Caesar's, and to God the things that are God's.

Day 23
Luke 23 – John 1

Terms to know
Paradise: A garden, park. In the New Testament, the abode of the blessed after death.

Risen: To rise, to rouse from sleep, sitting or death.

Messiah: Consecrated or anointed person, The Anointed One, the one promised from the beginning, the Christ.

Questions
1. What did Herod hope to see Jesus do?

2. What was to be preached in the name of Jesus?

3. Who is the "Word" in John 1:1-5?

Memory verse: John 1:12
But as many as received Him, to them He gave the right to become children of God, to those who believe in His name.

Day 24
John 2-4

Terms to know
Miracle: Sign, mark, token, supernatural act with a spiritual end and purpose.

Everlasting: Eternal, perpetual, belonging to the ages.

Savior: A deliverer, preserver, one who saves from danger or destruction and brings into a state of prosperity and happiness.

Questions
1. What did Jesus use to drive the money changers out of the temple?

2. Why do evil men hate the light?

3. What two things caused the people of the Samaritan city to believe in Jesus?

Memory verse: John 4:24
God is Spirit, and those who worship Him must worship in spirit and truth.

Day 25
John 5-7

Terms to know

Witness: One who bears record, to be able or ready to testify.

Manna: The miracle food the Israelites ate in the wilderness.

Feast of Tabernacles: The third great Jewish festival behind Passover and Pentecost. Held the 15th day of the 7th month and celebrated for 8 days.

Questions

1. Besides Jesus, what other witnesses are listed in John 5:31-39?

2. What caused some disciples to leave Jesus and not return?

3. How are we to judge?

Memory verse: John 6:38
For I have come down from heaven, not to do My own will, but the will of Him who sent Me.

Day 26
John 8-10

Terms to know

Truth: The reality, pertaining to the reality.

Put out of the Synagogue: Separated from the Synagogue, excommunicated. Exclusion from the fellowship, rights and privileges both civil and religious.

Hireling: One hired. Sometimes a hired person who shows no real interest in his duty and is unfaithful.

Questions

1. What do we become when we sin?

2. How did the formerly blind man refer to Jesus in John 9:11, 17, 33 and 38?

3. What does a hireling do in the face of danger and why?

Memory verse: John 9:4

I must work the works of Him who sent Me while it is day; the night is coming when no one can work.

Day 27
John 11-13

Terms to know

Wept: To shed tears, weep, shed a tear.

Lifted Up: To raise high, elevate. Seen in the brazen serpent as well as with Jesus foretelling of His crucifixion.

Girded: To bind about or around firmly. To firmly affix something around oneself.

Questions

1. How long had Lazarus been dead when Jesus brought him back to life?

2. Why did the Jews want to kill Lazarus?

3. How will people know the disciples of Jesus?

Memory verse: John 11:35
Jesus wept.

Day 28
John 14-16

Terms to know
Mansion: A residence, habitation, abode.

Abide: To remain, continue, tarry, dwell, live.

Helper: Paraclete, the Holy Spirit, comforter, advocate, intercessor, encourager, aid.

Questions
1. What does a person do who loves Jesus?

2. What did Jesus say is the greatest act of love?

3. What will some think as they kill a disciple of Jesus?

Memory verse: John 14:6
I am the way, the truth, and the life. No one comes to the Father except through Me.

End of Week 4

Congratulations on finishing another week of reading. Please use this page to write down people, events or teaching from the reading that you would like to learn more about. Share these with your family, small group, teacher or preacher and learn about them together.

For further study

Day 29
John 17-19

Terms to know
Manifested: Visible, conspicuous, to make apparent, known, show openly.

Detachment: A band, troop, company. A Roman detachment was probably a cohort, between 400-600. Also, a band from the guards of the temple.

Gabbatha: A raised or elevated place, tribunal, stage or scaffold.

Questions
1. Why did the world hate the disciples of Jesus?

2. Why did the Jews want the Romans to judge Jesus?

3. Who joined Joseph of Arimathea in preparing the body of Jesus?

Memory verse: John 19:2
And the soldiers twisted a crown of thorns and put it on His head, and they put on Him a purple robe.

Day 30
John 20 – Acts 1

Terms to know
Tomb: A sepulcher, a memorial or monument, a place of burial, grave. Often hewn out of rocks, hillsides or caverns.

Cubit: A measure equal to the length of a man's arm from the elbow to the end of his middle finger, about 21 inches.

Infallible Proofs: To mark out, a fixed sign, limit, goal. A fixed sign, certain or sure token.

Questions
1. What did Jesus show the disciples when He first appeared in the room?

2. How many times did Jesus ask Peter if he loved Him?

3. Who besides Matthias was considered to replace Judas as an apostle?

Memory verse: John 20:30-31
And truly Jesus did many other signs in the presence of His disciples, which are not written in this book; but these are written that you may believe that Jesus is the Christ, the Son of God, and that believing you may have life in His name.

Day 31
Acts 2-4

Terms to know

Pentecost: Fiftieth. One of the three great Jewish festivals in which all males were required to appear before God. Celebrated 50 days after the Passover. A festival of thanks for the harvest which began directly after the Passover.

Ninth Hour: According to Jewish reckoning, the ninth hour is 3 p.m., the hour of evening sacrifice and prayer.

Boldness: The act of speaking, freedom in speaking all that one thinks or pleases.

Questions

1. What two things did Peter tell the believing Jews to do?

2. How long had the lame man been lame?

3. What happened when new Christians were lacking?

Memory verse: Acts 2:41
Then those who gladly received his word were baptized; and that day about three thousand souls were added to them.

Day 32
Acts 5-7

Terms to know

Council: An assembly, joint session, Sanhedrin, the supreme council of the Jewish nation, composed of 70 members.

Proselyte: A stranger, foreigner, or one who comes from his own people to another. In the New Testament it is used for one converted from heathenism to Judaism.

Patriarch: The father and founder of a family or tribe.

Questions

1. What happed to the followers of Theudas and Judas of Galilee after their deaths?

2. Why did the apostles delegate the task of distributing food to widows?

3. What was Stephen's attitude toward those who were actively killing him?

Memory verse: Acts 5:29
We ought to obey God rather than men.

Day 33
Acts 8-10

Terms to know

Persecution: To follow, pursue. Hostile pursuit particularly of enemies.

Tanner: A leather dresser of a skin or hide of an animal, separated from the body

Centurion: A Roman military officer commanding one hundred men.

Questions
1. What was Simon's mistake in his request?

2. Why was Ananias reluctant to go see Saul?

3. How did Cornelius greet Peter?

Memory verse: Acts 10:34
Then Peter opened his mouth and said: "In truth I perceive that God shows no partiality."

Day 34
Acts 11-13

Terms to know

Unclean: Not fit by legal or ceremonial standards, unfit for rights and privileges, also referring to devils with unclean spirits.

Arrayed: To put on a garment, clothe oneself with something.

False Prophet: One who fraudulently assumes the work of a prophet when he pretends to foretell things to come.

Questions

1. How is Barnabas described?

2. What caused the death of Herod?

3. What was the punishment given to Elymas the sorcerer?

Memory verse: Acts 13:49
And the word of the Lord was being spread throughout all the region.

Day 35
Acts 14-16

Terms to know

Stoned: To pelt with stones or to stone to death.

Abstain: To keep oneself from, to refrain.

Seller of Purple: A female seller of purple cloths, a purple dealer.

Questions
1. What did the Jews of Antioch and Iconium do to Paul?

2. What did some want to bind on Gentile Christians in order to be saved?

3. Why did the jailer intend to kill himself?

Memory verse: Acts 14:23
So when they had appointed elders in every church, and prayed with fasting, they commended them to the Lord in whom they had believed.

End of Week 5

Congratulations on finishing another week of reading. Please use this page to write down people, events or teaching from the reading that you would like to learn more about. Share these with your family, small group, teacher or preacher and learn about them together.

For further study

Day 36
Acts 17-19

Terms to know
Noble: Good, well-born, noble-minded.

Tentmaker: A maker of tents.

Exorcist: Generally, one who by adjuration and incantation professes to expel demons, one who binds by an oath.

Questions
1. How are the Bereans described?

2. What did Aquila and Priscilla do with Apollos?

3. What did Demetrius do, and why was his livelihood in danger?

Memory verse: Acts 17:30
Truly, these times of ignorance God overlooked, but now commands all men everywhere to repent.

Day 37
Acts 20-22

Terms to know
Unleavened: Without corruption, metaphorically undefiled. Feast of the Passover is known as the Days of Unleavened Bread.

Evangelist: One who declares the good news, a preacher of the gospel, often not located in one place but as a missionary to establish churches in different places.

Zealous: To have the warmth of feeling for or against something; desire, covet, envy.

Questions
1. What was Paul's warning to the Ephesian elders?

2. What did Agabus foretell about Paul?

3. What did Paul declare that caused his scourging to cease?

Memory verse: Acts 22:16
And now why are you waiting? Arise and be baptized, and wash away your sins, calling on the name of the Lord.

Day 38
Acts 23-25

Terms to know
Conscience: To be one's own witness, regulator to one's own conduct in a moral sense.

Profane: To desecrate, to cross the threshold.

Judgment Seat: An elevated seat or throne upon which one in authority sits in judgment of others.

Questions
1. What were 40 Jews prepared to do to Paul?

2. What did Felix hope to receive from Paul?

3. How many charges against Paul were deserving of death?

Memory verse: Acts 24:25
Now as he reasoned about righteousness, self-control, and the judgment to come, Felix was afraid and answered, "Go away for now; when I have a convenient time I will call for you."

Day 39
Acts 26-28

Terms to know

Goads: To offer vain and rash resistance. A long stick with a pointed metal end to prod or goad cattle. To prick, stimulate.

Euroclydon: A tempestuous wind occurring on the Mediterranean, blown from all parts. It is violent and uncertain in course.

Sect: A form of religious worship, discipline or opinion.

Questions

1. What had Paul done earlier to Christians besides punishing them?

2. What warning did Paul give that was ignored?

3. What caused some to think that Paul was a god?

Memory verse: Acts 26:28
Then Agrippa said to Paul, "You almost persuade me to become a Christian."

Day 40
Romans 1-3

Terms to know
Righteousness: Justice, of actions, duties, equivalent to what is right, proper.

Anguish: Great distress, straits, distress arising from within.

Oracles: An orator, the declarations of God.

Questions
1. What was one reason Paul wished to visit the church in Rome?

2. What is in the future for the self-seeking unbelievers?

3. Where is our redemption found?

Memory verse: Romans 1:16
For I am not ashamed of the gospel of Christ, for it is the power of God to salvation for everyone who believes, for the Jew first and also for the Greek.

Day 41
Romans 4-6

Terms to know

Circumcision: To cut around, circumcise. A Jewish practice of foreskin removal, used also figuratively of persons practicing circumcision.

Reconciled: To change mutually, restore, redeem. The change God makes in man through conversion that he may be reconciled to God.

Dominion: To have or exercise rule or authority over, lord over.

Questions

1. How old was Abraham at the birth of Isaac, the son of promise?

2. How did God show His love to us?

3. What happened to our old man?

Memory verse: Romans 6:1-2

What shall we say then? Shall we continue in sin that grace may abound? Certainly not! How shall we who died to sin live any longer in it?

Day 42
Romans 7-9

Terms to know

Covet: To have the affections directed toward something, to lust, desire, long after.

Carnal: Fleshly as opposed to spiritual, implying sinfulness, proneness to sin.

Seed: Something sown and containing the germ of new fruit, of descendants.

Questions
1. What releases a wife from the bond to her husband?

2. What is not to be compared with the glory to be revealed in us?

3. If clay represents us, who does the potter represent?

Memory verse: Romans 8:28
And we know that all things work together for good to those who love God, to those who are called according to His purpose.

End of Week 6

Congratulations on finishing another week of reading. Please use this page to write down people, events or teaching from the reading that you would like to learn more about. Share these with your family, small group, teacher or preacher and learn about them together.

For further study

Day 43
Romans 10-12

Terms to know
Confess: to assent, concede, consent, admit, to profess openly of sins, of belief in Jesus as God.

Baal: Master, a heathen idol, the name of Phoenician and Babylonian god representing the sun or Jupiter.

Vengeance: To execute judgment, retribution, vindication, justice, punishment.

Questions
1. What was Paul's concern with Israel's zeal for God?

2. To whom was Paul an apostle?

3. What things should a Christian do to those who persecute, do evil or become an enemy?

Memory verse: Romans 12:18
If it is possible, as much as depends on you, live peaceably with all men.

Day 44
Romans 13-15

Terms to know
Authority: Permission, delegated influence, right to do something. Power over persons, things.

Contempt: Set at naught, to despise, treat with scorn, to reject with scorn.

Edification: The act of building up, building as a process.

Questions
1. To whom should Christians pay taxes?

2. Instead of a stumbling block, what should one pursue for others?

3. What was the purpose of things written in the past?

Memory verse: Romans 14:12
So then each of us shall give account of himself to God.

Day 45
Romans 16 – 1 Corinthians 2

Terms to know
Church: The called out, a congregation, assembly.

Stumbling Block: The trigger on a trap where the bait is placed. A cause of offending, falling, ruin, morally and spiritually.

Ordained: To determine or desire beforehand.

Questions
1. What should we do to those who cause divisions?

2. What is Christ crucified to Jews and Greeks?

3. How did Paul describe his speaking?

Memory verse: 1 Corinthians 1:10
Now I plead with you, brethren, by the name of our Lord Jesus Christ, that you all speak the same thing, and that there be no divisions among you, but that you be perfectly joined together in the same mind and in the same judgement.

Day 46
1 Corinthians 3-5

Terms to know

Defile: To corrupt, spoil, vitiate, in an amoral or spiritual sense.

Reviled: To vilify, reproach.

Puffed Up: To inflate, blow, pride, self-conceit, arrogant.

Questions

1. What is our only foundation upon which to build?

2. Who did Paul send to Corinth and for what reason?

3. What kinds of brothers are we to refrain from keeping company?

Memory verse: 1 Corinthians 3:9
For we are God's fellow workers; you are God's field, you are God's building.

Day 47
1 Corinthians 6-8

Terms to know

Sanctified: To make holy, to make clean, render pure, to consecrate, devote, set apart.

Divorce: To send forth or away, to put away, to let go.

Idol: An image or representation of some other thing. An image set up to be worshipped as a god.

Questions
1. What three things characterized the formerly sinful people who are now in Christ?

2. What was Paul's marital status?

3. What danger can our freedom or liberty cause in others?

Memory verse: 1 Corinthians 6:20
For you were bought at a price; therefore glorify God in your body and in your spirit, which are God's.

Day 48
1 Corinthians 9-11

Terms to know

Preach the Gospel: To evangelize, proclaim the good news, declare the gospel.

Profit: To bring together for the benefit of another, advantageous.

Unworthily: Irreverently, in an unbecoming manner.

Questions

1. Why was Paul willing to become different things to different people?

2. What two things will God do to protect a Christian from temptation?

3. What do we do each time we partake of the Lord's Supper?

Memory verse: 1 Corinthians 11:1
Imitate me, just as I also imitate Christ.

Day 49
1 Corinthians 12-14

Terms to know
Schism: To split, tear, divide as in mind or sentiment into factions.

Tongue: An organ of the body, of speech, language or dialect.

Exhortation: An act to beseech, encourage, comfort for the purpose of strengthening the faith of the believer.

Questions
1. Where did God place the members in the body?

2. What does love do?

3. God is the author of what?

Memory verse: 1 Corinthians 12:12
For as the body is one and has many members, but all the members of that one body, being many, are one body, so also is Christ.

End of Week 7

Congratulations on finishing another week of reading. Please use this page to write down people, events or teaching from the reading that you would like to learn more about. Share these with your family, small group, teacher or preacher and learn about them together.

For further study

Day 50
1 Corinthians 15 – 2 Corinthians 1

Terms to know

Resurrection: To stand up, raise to life again, recovery. In the New Testament, the resurrection of all the dead prior to the judgment.

Stand Fast: To stand firm in faith and duty for one's master and not for another.

Ignorant: To not perceive, understand, discern or recognize.

Questions

1. What is the impact to us if Jesus is still in the grave?

2. What awaited Paul along with the open door?

3. Who besides Paul had preached in Corinth?

Memory verse: 1 Corinthians 15:58
Therefore, my beloved brethren, be steadfast, immovable, always abounding in the work of the Lord, knowing that your labor is not in vain in the Lord.

Day 51
2 Corinthians 2-4

Terms to know
Grieved: To distress, afflict with sorrow, to be sad, sorrowful.

Commend: To cause to stand with, to introduce, present to someone for favorable notice, worthy.

Veiled: To envelop, wrap around, to hide, to cover over.

Questions
1. Why did Paul have no rest in his spirit?

2. What causes the veil to be taken away?

3. What does our light affliction produce?

Memory verse: 2 Corinthians 4:7
But we have this treasure in earthen vessels, that the excellence of the power may be of God and not of us.

Day 52
2 Corinthians 5-7

Terms to know
Ambassador: An aged person, elderly, representing someone.

Stripe: A stroke, stripe, blow, wound or injury.

Perfecting: To finish, complete, finish to the full end.

Questions
1. What did Jesus become for us?

2. What warning did Paul give concerning unbelievers?

3. What does godly sorrow produce?

Memory verse: 2 Corinthians 5:20
Now then, we are ambassadors for Christ, as though God were pleading through us: we implore you on Christ's behalf, be reconciled to God.

Day 53
2 Corinthians 8-10

Terms to know
Diligent: Earnest, prompt, more diligent, forward.

Superfluous: Over and above, more than enough, exceeding a certain measure.

Meekness: Gentle, humble, mild. Does not denote outward expression of feeling but an inward peace of the soul, calmness.

Questions
1. How long had the Corinthian church been planning their giving to Paul's needs?

2. What can God's grace produce in us for all things and good works?

3. How did others describe Paul's letters, bodily presence and speech?

Memory verse: 2 Corinthians 9:7
So let each one give as he purposes in his heart, not grudgingly or of necessity; for God loves a cheerful giver.

Day 54
2 Corinthians 11-13

Terms to know
False Apostle: One who pretends to be an apostle of Christ.

Buffet: To strike with the fist, to mistreat.

Disqualified: Unapproved, unworthy, spurious, worthless, rejected, disapproved, cast away.

Questions
1. Into what can Satan transform himself?

2. What did the thorn in the flesh allow Paul to do?

3. What should we do to see if we are disqualified?

Memory verse: 2 Corinthians 13:12
Greet one another with a holy kiss.

Day 55
Galatians 1-3

Terms to know
Accursed: Anathema, a gift or vow devoted to destruction for God's sake. Given up to the curse and destruction.

Gentiles: A people, race, belonging and living together, inhabitants of Samaria, in the Jewish sense all nations who are not Israelites.

Tutor: An instructor or teacher of children, an educator, a schoolmaster.

Questions
1.   How did Paul receive the gospel?

2.   Why did Paul confront Peter to his face?

3.   By what action does one put on Christ?

Memory verse: Galatians 2:20
I have been crucified with Christ; it is no longer I who live, but Christ lives in me; and the life which I now live in the flesh I live by faith in the Son of God, who loved me and gave Himself for me.

Day 56
Galatians 4-6

Terms to know
Covenant: To set out in order, to dispose to a certain order, testament. A solemn disposition, institution from God to man.

Liberty: Freedom, generosity, independence.

Trespass: To fall by the wayside, fault, lapse, error, mistake, wrongdoing.

Questions
1. What would the people have done for Paul in his infirmity?

2. What are the elements of the fruit of the Spirit?

3. What two conditions are mentioned for the one restoring a sinning brother?

Memory verse: Galatians 6:9
And let us not grow weary while doing good, for in due season we shall reap if we do not lose heart.

End of Week 8

Congratulations on finishing another week of reading. Please use this page to write down people, events or teaching from the reading that you would like to learn more about. Share these with your family, small group, teacher or preacher and learn about them together.

For further study

Day 57
Ephesians 1-3

Terms to know
Predestined: To determine or decree beforehand.

Grace: Causes joy, gratification, acceptance, a favor done without expectation of return, unearned and unmerited favor.

Mystery: Something hidden and not fully manifested.

Questions
1. Through what do we have redemption?

2. As His workmanship, what are we created to do?

3. What was the mystery Paul spoke of in Ephesians 3:6?

Memory verse: Ephesians 2:8
For by grace you have been saved through faith, and that not of yourselves; it is the gift of God.

Day 58
Ephesians 4-6

Terms to know
Unity: Oneness, unanimity.

Imitators: A follower.

Eyeservice: Implying either service rendered only when one is being scrutinized, or service rendered only for appearance sake.

Questions
1. Rather than corrupt words, what should proceed out of our mouths?

2. How should husbands love their wives?

3. What are the pieces of the armor of God?

Memory verse: Ephesians 4:32
And be kind to one another, tenderhearted, forgiving one another, even as God in Christ forgave you.

Day 59
Philippians 1-3

Terms to know
Bishop: A watchman, overseer, superintendent, officer in the local church, elder.

Selfish Ambition: Self-conceited, empty pride, desire for praise.

Pattern: A mark, print, impression, form, a prototype, model.

Questions
1. Of what should our conduct be worthy?

2. How are we to esteem others?

3. Where is our citizenship as Christians?

Memory verse: Philippians 1:21
For to me, to live is Christ, and to die is gain.

Day 60
Philippians 4 – Colossians 2

Terms to know

Rejoice: To be glad, well-off, cheerful.

Preeminence: To be first, chief, to hold the first rank, highest dignity.

Philosophy: Love of wisdom, which came to mean the doctrine or tenants of the heathen or gentile philosophers.

Questions

1. Upon what things should we meditate?

2. From what has Jesus delivered us?

3. What did Jesus do to the handwriting of requirements against us?

Memory verse: Philippians 4:13
I can do all things through Christ who strengthens me.

Day 61
Colossians 3 – 1 Thessalonians 1

Terms to know
Malice: Wickedness as an evil habit of the mind, to do evil to others.

Epistle: To send a letter or enjoin by writing. A letter or written message, a letter of authority.

Election: To choose, select, a chosen vessel, an instrument of usefulness.

Questions
1. As Christians, what things are we to put off?

2. What instructions did Paul give about epistle reading?

3. What three things did Paul remember without ceasing about the Thessalonians?

Memory verse: Colossians 4:6
Let your speech always be with grace, seasoned with salt, that you may know how you ought to answer each one.

Day 62
1 Thessalonians 2-4

Terms to know

Vain: Empty, fruitless, meaningless, aimlessness, absence of good.

Blameless: Without fault, above reproach, without fault.

Sanctification: Separation unto God, holiness.

Questions

1. What charge as a father to children did Paul give the Thessalonians?

2. Who did Paul send to establish and encourage the church?

3. What 5 goals are listed for us in 1 Thessalonians 4:11-12?

Memory verse: 1 Thessalonians 4:7
For God did not call us to uncleanness, but in holiness.

Day 63
1 Thessalonians 5 – 2 Thessalonians 2

Terms to know
Quench: To go out, extinguish as with a fire, to hinder the Holy Spirit.

Gospel: Good news, glad tidings, the salvation through Christ.

Perdition: To destroy fully, the state of death apart from salvation, an allusion to the antichrist, one who is eternally lost.

Questions
1. How will the day of the Lord come?

2. Upon whom will vengeance be taken?

3. Through what did God call us to obtain the glory of Jesus?

Memory verse: 1 Thessalonians 5:16-18
Rejoice always, pray without ceasing, in everything give thanks; for this is the will of God in Christ Jesus for you.

End of Week 9

Congratulations on finishing another week of reading. Please use this page to write down people, events or teaching from the reading that you would like to learn more about. Share these with your family, small group, teacher or preacher and learn about them together.

For further study

Day 64
2 Thessalonians 3 – 1 Timothy 2

Terms to know
Admonish: To warn, caution, reprove gently, exhort.

Fable: A tale, fabrication by the mind in contrast to reality, falsehood.

Supplication: To make known one's particular need, prayer for a particular benefit.

Questions
1. How were the non-working, disorderly members described?

2. What was Paul prior to being in the ministry of Jesus?

3. What is one stated reason why Christians should pray for all in authority?

Memory verse: 1 Timothy 2:5-6
For there is one God and one Mediator between God and men, the Man Christ Jesus, who gave Himself a ransom for all to be testified in due time.

Day 65
1 Timothy 3-5

Terms to know
Novice: Newly sprung up, one lately converted to Christianity or new in the church.

Meditate: To be of interest, to consider, weigh, ponder over something.

Gossip: To boil, bubble up with heat, an idle or trifling talker, one who boils over with impertinent talk.

Questions
1. Why should a bishop (overseer, elder) be one who rules his own house well?

2. How was Timothy encouraged to be an example?

3. How is one described who does not provide for his own household?

Memory verse: 1 Timothy 4:16
Take heed to yourself and to the doctrine. Continue in them, for in doing this you will save both yourself and those who hear you.

Day 66
1 Timothy 6 – 2 Timothy 2

Terms to know

Potentate: Possessor of power or authority, one who occupies high position.

Preacher: Herald, proclaimer, one who is employed by God in the work of proclaiming salvation.

Iniquity: Wrong, injustice, impropriety, unrighteousness, wickedness.

Questions

1. What is a root of all kinds of evil?

2. Who was instrumental in Timothy's early spiritual training?

3. What qualities should a servant of the Lord possess?

Memory verse: 1 Timothy 6:6
Now godliness with contentment is great gain.

Day 67
2 Timothy 3 – Titus 1

Terms to know
Reproof: To convince, persuade, refute adversaries.

Longsuffering: Forbearance, restraint before proceeding with action. The quality of a person who is able to avenge himself yet refrains from doing so.

Hospitable: A friend or lover of strangers, kind to strangers, guests.

Questions
1. What had Timothy carefully followed?

2. Who forsook Paul and why?

3. Why did Paul leave Titus in Crete?

Memory verse: 2 Timothy 4:2
Preach the word! Be ready in season and out of season. Convince, rebuke, exhort with all longsuffering and teaching.

Day 68
Titus 2 – Philemon 1

Terms to know
Sober: Temperate, self-controlled, especially in regard to wine. The state of mind which is free from excessive influences of passion, lust or emotion.

Regeneration: Spiritual renovation, spiritual rebirth.

Compulsion: Necessity, compelling forces as opposed to willingness.

Questions
1. Why would an opponent of a spiritual young man be ashamed?

2. What things are listed as profitable and unprofitable?

3. What had been refreshed by Philemon?

Memory verse: Titus 3:1-2
Remind them to be subject to rulers and authorities, to obey, to be ready for every good work, to speak evil of no one, to be peaceable, gentle, showing all humility to all men.

Day 69
Hebrews 1-3

Terms to know

Inheritance: To be an heir to, obtain by inheritance a possession.

Confidence: Freedom, frankness, boldness, particularly in speaking, outspoken, assured.

Drift Away: To float by as a ship, to slip away suggesting a gradual and unnoticed movement past a certain point. To glide away, to swerve or deviate from truth, law or faith.

Questions

1. Where did Jesus sit down?

2. What is the danger if one forgets what he heard?

3. What prevented the people in the wilderness from entering into God's rest?

Memory verse: Hebrews 3:12-13
Beware, brethren, lest there be in any of you an evil heart of unbelief in departing from the living God; but exhort one another daily, while it is called "Today," lest any of you be hardened through the deceitfulness of sin.

Day 70
Hebrews 4-6

Terms to know
Sympathize: To commiserate, have compassion upon.

Discern: To discern, decide, judge, distinguish.

Heir: Getting by appointment, a possessor of inheritance divided by lot.

Questions
1. What does the word of God discern?

2. Jesus is the author of what and for whom?

3. What is impossible for God to do?

Memory verse: Hebrews 4:12
For the word of God is living and powerful, and sharper than any two-edged sword, piercing even to the division of soul and spirit, and of joints and marrow, and is a discerner of the thoughts and intents of the heart.

Day 71
Hebrews 7-9

Terms to know
Tithe: A portion, a tenth part, Jewish requirement to pay a tenth of increase of produce and flocks.

Mediator: One who goes between two parties, a reconciler.

Testator: To arrange and dispose of one's effects by will and testament.

Questions
1. What titles or positions did Melchizedek have?

2. Where is our High Priest?

3. When is a testament in force?

End of Week 10

Congratulations on finishing another week of reading. Please use this page to write down people, events or teaching from the reading that you would like to learn more about. Share these with your family, small group, teacher or preacher and learn about them together.

For further study

Day 72
Hebrews 10-12

Terms to know
Shadow: Shade, metaphorically, a foreshadowing, the Jewish rites were a shadow of greater things to come in Christ.

Faith: Firm persuasion, conviction, belief in the truth.

Chastening: Correction, rectification, discipline, such training as the Lord approves.

Questions
1. What could the blood of bulls and goats not do?

2. What did Abraham believe God would do when he offered his son of promise?

3. What are the benefits of chastening or discipline?

Memory verse: Hebrews 11:6
But without faith it is impossible to please Him, for he who comes to God must believe that He is and that He is a rewarder of those who diligently seek Him.

90

Day 73
Hebrews 13 – James 2

Terms to know
Doctrine: To teach, instruct, tutor, the teachings of a person.

Enticed: To bait, entrap, allure, beguile.

Partiality: A respecting of persons, favoritism.

Questions
1. What should we do to those who lead and rule over us?

2. What is the difference in a hearer and a doer?

3. What is faith without works?

Memory verse: James 1:19
So then my beloved brethren, let every man be swift to hear, slow to speak, slow to wrath.

Day 74
James 3-5

Terms to know

Hypocrisy: To pretend, simulate, originally it meant inexperienced in the art of acting.

Enmity: Hostility a reason for opposition, hatred.

Sabaoth: Lord of Hosts, of angelic hosts, Jehovah omnipotent, all-ruling, almighty.

Questions

1. What resides with envy and self-seeking?

2. What should we do with our hearts as we draw near to God?

3. What was the effect of the prayers of Elijah?

Memory verse: James 5:16
Confess your trespasses to one another, and pray for one another, that you may be healed. The effective, fervent prayer of a righteous man avails much.

Day 75
1 Peter 1-3

Terms to know

Foreknowledge: To know beforehand, prior acknowledgment, favorable recognition or consideration in advance.

Shepherd: One who generally cares for the flocks, locally an elder in the church to watch over and provide for the welfare of the church. Jesus is the great shepherd.

Antitype: A model, figure, implies resemblance, counterpart, correspondence.

Questions

1. How does the Father judge?

2. Besides God's special people, how does Peter describe the Christian?

3. What might hinder the prayers of husbands?

Memory verse: 1 Peter 1:3

Blessed be the God and Father of our Lord Jesus Christ, who according to His abundant mercy has begotten us again to a living hope through the resurrection of Jesus Christ from the dead.

Day 76
1 Peter 4 – 2 Peter 1

Terms to know
Ashamed: To shame oneself, put to shame, be dishonored.

Humble: Low, not high, particularly of attitude and social position.

Virtue: Moral excellence, perfection, goodness in action.

Questions
1. What two things should one do who suffers as a Christian?

2. What negative commands does Peter give to elders concerning how they shepherd the flock?

3. What are the things a Christian should add in order to never stumble?

Memory verse: 1 Peter 5:6-7
Therefore humble yourselves under the mighty hand of God, that He may exalt you in due time, casting all your care upon Him, for He cares for you.

Day 77
2 Peter 2 – 1 John 1

Terms to know

Exploit: Going about as a merchant or trader, intending to trade for profit, a deceiver for one's own gain.

Salvation: A savior, deliverer, deliverance, preservation from dangers or destruction. Deliverance from sin and spiritual consequences through Jesus Christ.

Joy: Calm delight, gladness, cheerfulness.

Questions

1. How does Peter describe a believer who returns to the ways of the world?

2. How does the longsuffering (patience) of the Lord affect our repentance?

3. How would you contrast walking in light and walking in darkness in 1 John 1?

Memory verse: 1 John 1:9
If we confess our sins, He is faithful and just to forgive us our sins and to cleanse us from all unrighteousness.

End of Week 11

Congratulations on finishing another week of reading. Please use this page to write down people, events or teaching from the reading that you would like to learn more about. Share these with your family, small group, teacher or preacher and learn about them together.

For further study

Day 78
1 John 2-4

Terms to know

Propitiation: To atone, expiate, the benefit of Christ's blood for the sinner. Jesus to pay the price of sins to reconcile with God.

Devil: A false accuser, slanderer, Satan.

Love: Agape, affection, regard, goodwill, benevolence, love of neighbor, brotherly affection, the love that is derived from God.

Questions

1. How does John describe antichrist?

2. Besides our speech, how should Christians demonstrate love?

3. Why is it wrong to say one loves God while hating his brother?

Memory verse: 1 John 2:3
Now by this we know that we know Him, if we keep His commandments.

Day 79
1 John 5 – 3 John 1

Terms to know

Petition: A thing asked or an asking, particular requests in prayer.

Antichrist: An opposer of Christ, one who usurps the place of Christ, all who deny Jesus is messiah and is come in the flesh.

Prating: To overflow with talk, chatter, prattle, talking idly or falsely.

Questions

1. Why did John write these things?

2. How does John describe love?

3. What was John's greatest joy?

Memory verse: 3 John 1:4
I have no greater joy than to hear that my children walk in truth.

Day 80
Jude 1 – Revelation 2

Terms to know

Contend: To strive, struggle earnestly, to fight for something.

Tribulation: To crush, press, squeeze, compress, break, trouble, pressure from evils, affliction, distress.

Nicolaitans: An ancient sect whose deeds were expressly and strongly reprobate.

Questions

1. Why did Jude feel it necessary to write exhorting to contend for the faith?

2. What terms describe the Alpha and Omega?

3. What did Jesus hold against the church at Ephesus?

Memory verse: Revelation 1:3
Blessed is he who reads and those who hear the words of this prophecy, and keep those things which are written in it; for the time is near.

Day 81
Revelation 3-4

Terms to know
Worthy: To weigh, an estimate of values, of equal value, useful, deserving, suitable.

Holy: Separation, consecration, devotion to the service of God, abstaining from defilement and sharing in the purity of God.

Questions
1. What does Jesus want the church at Laodicea to do when rebuked?

2. How many wings each did the four living creatures have?

Memory verse: Revelation 2:29
He who has an ear, let him hear what the Spirit says to the churches.

Day 82
Revelation 5-6

Terms to know
Lamb: Designation of the exalted Christ.

Seal: To close up, to keep secure, a stamp or mark of authority.

Questions
1. Who was not able or worthy to open the scroll?

2. What were the colors of the four horses?

Memory verse: Revelation 5:13b
Blessing and honor and glory and power
Be to the one who sits on the throne,
And to the Lamb, forever and ever!

Day 83
Revelation 7-8

Terms to know
Angel: Messenger, one who is sent to announce or proclaim, a celestial messenger.

Censer: An incense vessel or censer.

Questions
1. How many were sealed from each tribe and what was the total of all 12 tribes?

2. What ascended to God with the smoke of the incense?

Memory verse: Revelation 7:11-12
All of the angels stood around the throne and the elders and the four living creatures, and fell on their faces before the throne and worshiped God, saying,
"Amen!
Blessing and glory and wisdom,
Thanksgiving and honor and power and might,
Be to our God forever and ever. Amen!"

Day 84
Revelation 9-10

Terms to know

Plague: A stroke, a blow inflicted by God, a calamity.

Little Book: A small roll or volume, a little scroll.

Questions

1. What name was given to the angel of the bottomless pit?

2. What did John do with the little book?

Memory verse: Revelation 10:11

And he said to me, "You must prophesy again about many peoples, nations, tongues, and kings.

End of Week 12

Congratulations on finishing another week of reading. Please use this page to write down people, events or teaching from the reading that you would like to learn more about. Share these with your family, small group, teacher or preacher and learn about them together.

For further study

Day 85
Revelation 11-12

Terms to know

Sackcloth: Coarse black cloth commonly made of the long hair of goats. Used for straining, for sacks and for mourning garments in place of normal garments.

Woe: Of denouncing misery and pitying it.

Questions

1. How long will the two witnesses prophesy?

2. Who fought the war with the dragon?

Memory verse: Revelation 12:9

So the great dragon was cast out, that serpent of old, called the Devil and Satan, who deceives the whole world; he was cast to the earth, and his angels were cast out with him.

Day 86
Revelation 13-14

Terms to know

Beast: Predominantly used of lower animal life, a dangerous or venomous creature or beasts in general.

Redeemed: to buy a thing, bought at a price. Christ purchased the saved through His sacrifice.

Questions

1. What did the beast of the earth cause all to receive and where?

2. What was on the foreheads of the 144,000?

Memory verse: Revelation 14:13

Then I heard a voice from heaven saying to me, "Write: Blessed are the dead who die in the Lord from now on," "Yes," says the Spirit, "that they may rest from their labors, and their works follow them."

Day 87
Revelation 15-16

Terms to know
Temple: A dwelling, a place of worship symbolically of the temple of God in heaven.

Armageddon: Megiddo, a place of destruction or slaughter in the Old Testament. A place for the overthrow of Satan.

Questions
1. How were the seven angels clothed?

2. What were the seven plagues from the seven bowls?

Memory verse: Revelation 16:15
Behold I am coming as a thief. Blessed is he who watches, and keeps his garments, lest he walk naked and they see his shame.

Day 88
Revelation 17-18

Terms to know

Martyr: A witness who can give testimony. Those who have suffered death in consequence of confessing Christ.

Babylon: The capital of Chaldea, symbolic name for heathen Rome who took the place of ancient Babylon as a persecuting power.

Questions
1. On what was the woman, the great harlot, drunk?

2. What had fallen Babylon become and what did it contain?

Memory verse: Revelation 17:14
These will make war with the Lamb, and the Lamb will overcome them, for He is Lord of lords, King of kings; and those who are with Him are called, chosen and faithful.

Day 89
Revelation 19-20

Terms to know

Alleluia: An adoring exclamation, Praise God!

Satan: The opposer, adversary, devil.

Questions

1. How was the man who sat on the white horse described?

2. By what are the dead judged?

Memory verse: Revelation 20:15
And anyone not found written in the Book of Life was cast into the lake of fire.

Day 90
Revelation 21-22

Terms to know

Abomination: To emit a foul odor, disgust, abhor, that which is detestable to God, unclean, impure.

Amen: To be firm steady, trustworthy, affirmation in the truth, verily it is so. Also means consent or desire, so be it, and as such it concludes prayers.

Questions

1. Who all will have their part in the lake of fire?

2. What happens to those who add to or take away from the book of prophecy?

Memory verse: Revelation 21:4

And God shall wipe away every tear from their eyes; there shall be no more death, nor sorrow, nor crying. There shall be no more pain, for the former things have passed away.

End of Week 13

Congratulations on finishing another week of reading. Please use this page to write down people, events or teaching from the reading that you would like to learn more about. Share these with your family, small group, teacher or preacher and learn about them together.

For further study

List of words with Strong's numbers

The terms defined in this reading plan are keyed to Strong's numbers. This relates to a standard lexicon, or dictionary organization for the terms. Some words used in this plan have multiple meanings. The reader may wish to do some additional research based on these numbers to learn more about the terms.

A
Abides - 3306
Abomination - 946
Abstain - 567
Admonish - 3560
Adultery - 3429
Adversary - 480
Alleluia - 239
Alms - 1654
Ambassador - 4243
Amen - 181
Angel - 32
Anguish - 4730
Anointed - 5548
Antichrist - 500
Antitype - 499
Apostle - 652
Armageddon - 717
Arrayed - 1746
Ashamed - 153
Austere - 840
Authority - 1849

B
Baal - 896
Babylon - 897
Baptize - 907

Beast - 2342
Beelzebub - 954
Betrothed - 3423
Bishop - 1985
Blameless - 273
Blasphemy - 988
Blessed - 3107
Boldness - 3954
Buffet - 2852

C
Carnal - 4561
Carousing - 2897
Censer - 3031
Centurion - 1543
Chastening - 3809
Christ - 5547
Church - 1577
Circumcision – 4061
Commend - 4921
Compulsion - 318
Confess - 3670
Confidence - 3954
Conscience - 4893
Contempt - 1848
Contend - 1864
Corban - 2878

Cornerstone - 1137
Council - 4892
Covenant - 1242
Covet - 1937
Covetousness - 4124
Crucified - 4717
Cubit - 4083

D
Deceive - 4105
Defile - 5351
Demon - 1142
Denarius - 1220
Detachment - 4686
Devil - 1228
Diligent - 4705
Discern - 1253
Disciple - 3101
Disqualified - 96
Divorce - 863
Doctrine - 1322
Dominion - 2961
Drift Away - 3901
Dropsy - 5203

E
Edification - 3619
Election - 1589
Enmity - 2189
Enticed - 1185
Epistle - 1992
Euoclydon - 2148
Evangelist - 2099
Everlasting - 166
Exhortation - 3874
Exorcist - 1845
Exploit - 1710
Eyeservice - 3787

F
Fable - 3454
Faith - 4102
False Apostle 5570
False Prophet - 5578
Fast - 3522
Feast of Tabernacles - 4634
Foreknowledge - 4268
Forgive - 863

G
Gabbatha -1042
Genealogy - 1078
Gentiles - 1484
Girded - 1241
Glutton - 5314
Goads - 2759
Gospel - 2098
Gossip - 5397
Grace – 4584
Grieved - 3076

H
Heir - 2818
Helper - 3875
Hireling - 3411
Holy - 40
Hosanna - 5614
Hospitable - 5382
Humble - 5011
Hypocrisy - 505

I
Idol -1497
Ignorant – 50
Imitator -3402
Implore - 1189
Infallible Proofs - 5039

Inheritance - 2816
Iniquity – 93

J
Joy - 5479
Judgment Seat - 968
Justified - 1344

L
Lamb - 721
Leper - 3015
Liberty - 1657
Lifted Up - 5312
Little Book - 974
Longsuffering - 3115
Love - 26

M
Magi - 3097
Malice - 2549
Manifested - 5319
Manna - 3131
Mansion - 3438
Martyr - 3144
Mediator - 3316
Meditate - 3191
Meekness - 4236
Merciful - 3629
Messiah - 3323
Millstone - 3037/3457
Miracle - 4592
Mite - 3016
Mystery – 3466

N
Ninth Hour – 1766
Nicolaitans - 3531
Nobel - 2104

Novice – 3504

O
Offend - 4624
Oracles - 3501
Ordained - 4309

P
Parable - 3850
Paradise - 3857
Paralytic - 3885
Partiality - 4382
Passover - 3957
Patriarch - 3966
Pattern - 5179
Pentecost - 4005
Perdition - 684
Perfecting - 2005
Perishing - 622
Persecution - 1375
Persistence - 335
Petition - 155
Pharisee - 5330
Philosophy – 5385
Phylacteries - 5440
Plague - 4127
Potentate - 1413
Praetorium - 4232
Prating - 5396
Preach the Gospel - 2097
Preacher - 2783
Predestined - 4309
Preeminence - 4409
Prodigal - 811
Profane - 953
Profit - 4851
Prophesied - 4395
Propitiation - 2434

Proselyte - 4339
Publican - 5057
Puffed up - 5448
Put out of Synagogue - 656

Q
Quench - 4570

R
Rabbi - 4461
Rebuked - 3679
Reconciled - 2644
Redeemed - 59
Regeneration - 3824
Rejoice - 5463
Remission - 859
Repentance - 3341
Reproof - 1650
Resurrection - 386
Reviled - 3058
Righteousness - 1343
Risen - 1453

S
Sabbath - 4521
Saboath - 4519
Sackcloth - 4526
Sadducee - 4523
Salvation - 4991
Samaritan - 4541
Sanctification - 38
Sanctified - 37
Satan - 4567
Savior - 4990
Schism - 4978
Scribe - 1122
Seal - 4973
Sect - 139

Seed - 4690
Selfish Ambition - 2754
Seller of Purple - 4211
Sexual Immorality - 4202
Shadow - 4639
Shepherd - 4166
Sign - 4592
Sober - 3524
Stand fast - 4739
Steward - 3623
Stoned - 3036
Stripe - 4127
Stumbling Block - 4625
Superfluous - 4053
Supplication - 1162
Sympathize - 4834
Synagogue - 4864

T
Talent - 5007
Tanner - 1038
Temple - 3845
Tempt - 1598
Tentmaker - 4635
Testator - 1303
Tetrarch - 5076
Tithe - 1181
Tomb - 3419
Tongue - 1100
Transfigured - 3339
Transgress - 3845
Trespass - 3900
Tribulation - 2347
Truth - 225
Tutor - 3807

U
Unclean - 169

Unity - 1775
Unleavened Bread - 106
Unworthily - 371

V
Vain - 2756
Veiled - 2572
Vengeance - 1557
Virtue - 703

W
Wayside - 3598

Wept - 1145
Witness - 3140
Woe - 3579
Work - 1411
Worthy - 514

Y
Yoke – 2218

Z
Zealous - -2207

About 90DayBiblePlan.com

Our goal is to provide resources to assist more people in good Bible reading habits. The 90-day Bible format will be used in 4 additional volumes covering Law, History, Wisdom and Prophets of the Old Testament.

Visit 90DayBiblePlan.com to receive free lesson ideas and class outlines that complement the readings of the New Testament.

www.90DayBiblePlan.com

90 Day New Testament Reading Plan
90DayBiblePlan.com

- ❑ 1. Matt. 1-3
- ❑ 2. Matt. 4-6
- ❑ 3. Matt. 7-9
- ❑ 4. Matt. 10-12
- ❑ 5. Matt. 13-15
- ❑ 6. Matt. 16-18
- ❑ 7. Matt. 19-21
- ❑ 8. Matt. 22-24
- ❑ 9. Matt. 25-27
- ❑ 10. Matt. 28 - Mark 2
- ❑ 11. Mark 3-5
- ❑ 12. Mark 6-8
- ❑ 13. Mark 9-11
- ❑ 14. Mark 12-14
- ❑ 15. Mark 15 - Luke 1
- ❑ 16. Luke 2-4
- ❑ 17. Luke 5-7
- ❑ 18. Luke 8-10
- ❑ 19. Luke 11-13
- ❑ 20. Luke 14-16
- ❑ 21. Luke 17-19
- ❑ 22. Luke 20-22
- ❑ 23. Luke 23 - John 1
- ❑ 24. John 2-4
- ❑ 25. John 5-7
- ❑ 26. John 8-10
- ❑ 27. John 11-13
- ❑ 28. John 14-16
- ❑ 29. John 17-19
- ❑ 30. John 20 - Acts 1
- ❑ 31. Acts 2-4
- ❑ 32. Acts 5-7
- ❑ 33. Acts 8-10
- ❑ 34. Acts 11-13
- ❑ 35. Acts 14-16
- ❑ 36. Acts 17-19
- ❑ 37. Acts 20-22
- ❑ 38. Acts 23-25
- ❑ 39. Acts 26-28
- ❑ 40. Rom. 1-3
- ❑ 41. Rom. 4-6
- ❑ 42. Rom. 7-9
- ❑ 43. Rom. 10-12
- ❑ 44. Rom. 13-15
- ❑ 45. Rom. 16 - 1 Cor. 2
- ❑ 46. 1 Cor. 3-5
- ❑ 47. 1 Cor. 6-8
- ❑ 48. 1 Cor. 9-11
- ❑ 49. 1 Cor. 12-14
- ❑ 50. 1 Cor. 15 - 2 Cor. 1
- ❑ 51. 2 Cor. 2-4
- ❑ 52. 2 Cor. 5-7
- ❑ 53. 2 Cor. 8-10
- ❑ 54. 2 Cor. 11-13
- ❑ 55. Gal. 1-3
- ❑ 56. Gal. 4-6
- ❑ 57. Eph. 1-3
- ❑ 58. Eph. 4-6
- ❑ 59. Phil. 1-3
- ❑ 60. Phil. 4-Col. 2
- ❑ 61. Col. 3-1 Thess. 1
- ❑ 62. 1 Thess. 2-4
- ❑ 63. 1 Thess. 5 - 2 Thess. 2
- ❑ 64. 2 Thess. 3 - 1 Tim. 2
- ❑ 65. 1 Tim. 3-5
- ❑ 66. 1 Tim. 6 - 2 Tim. 2
- ❑ 67. 2 Tim. 3 - Titus 1
- ❑ 68. Titus 2 - Philemon 1
- ❑ 69. Heb. 1-3
- ❑ 70. Heb. 4-6
- ❑ 71. Heb. 7-9
- ❑ 72. Heb. 10-12
- ❑ 73. Heb. 13 - Jas. 2
- ❑ 74. Jas. 3-5
- ❑ 75. 1 Pet. 1-3
- ❑ 76. 1 Pet. 2 - 2 Pet. 1
- ❑ 77. 2 Pet. 2 - 1 John 1
- ❑ 78. 1 John 2-4
- ❑ 79. 1 John 5 - 3 John 1
- ❑ 80. Jude 1 - Rev. 2
- ❑ 81. Rev. 3-4
- ❑ 82. Rev. 5-6
- ❑ 83. Rev. 7-8
- ❑ 84. Rev. 9-10
- ❑ 85. Rev. 11-12
- ❑ 86. Rev. 13-14
- ❑ 87. Rev. 15-16
- ❑ 88. Rev. 17-18
- ❑ 89. Rev. 19-20
- ❑ 90. Rev. 21-22